Hey God!

Peter St John

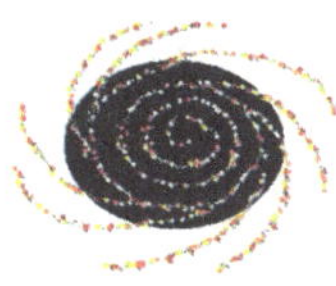

Published in 2015 by the author
using SilverWood Books Empowered Publishing ®

SilverWood Books
14 Small Street, Bristol, BS1 1DE
www.silverwoodbooks.co.uk

Readers should note that the author has taken good-natured liberties with grammar and punctuation because this suits the tone and setting of the book.

ISBN 978-1-78132-396-0

British Library Cataloguing in Publication Data
A CIP catalogue record for this book is available from the British Library

Set in Palatino by SilverWood Books
Printed on responsibly sourced paper

SilverWood

"Get out of the box. Open your mind and imagination and enjoy this serious yet often humorous discussion between a man and God as the man asks about life, death, heaven and hell, and truly, God knows what else.

If you are locked in dogma, you won't like this book. If you are open to theological 'what ifs'...you will love it. As a rabbi and a chaplain, I found witnessing this discussion profound, thought provoking and fun."

– Anne White, www.creatingcalmnetwork.com

"It's easy to read, well-written and thought provoking. This booklet will make you laugh and ponder... and is very likely to challenge your beliefs. I was given this as a gift and thoroughly enjoyed it! It made me realize what I have missed by spending all these years barely reading any books (because of having been forced at school to read, which led to me reading books that weren't well-written and thought-provoking enough to my liking).

A delight to read, this booklet, containing a fictional conversation between a man and God (or, perhaps, his imagination?), sure is worth a read!

While some might feel offended reading this book, I think the philosophical value will still make it worth the purchase for those people as well.

If you like pondering on philosophical and theological subjects, you will not be disappointed if you add this booklet to your collection!"

– Didier Strijdonk, www.goodreads.com

Peter St John is best known for his six "Gang" books about children's gangs during World War II. These novels spring from adventures in an English village as an evacuee from the London Blitz.

Two other novels draw on his career as a chartered engineer in aerospace research, as well as from experience within parliamentary and governmental organisations.

An occasional poem of his has been published.

He lives in France where he is active in a cultural association.

By the same author:

"Gang Territory"
"Gang Warfare"
"Gang Rivalry"
"Gang Loyalty
"Gang Petition"
"Gang Spies"
"Siberian Summer"
"Triple Agent"
and
"Jenno's Gangs"

Details may be found at www.peterstjohn.net

Acknowledgements

Warm thanks are due (in alphabetical order) to:

Alter Ego for inspiration
Anne-Lise Brugger Grataloup for conspiration
Catherine Loew for amelioration
Ego for application
Erika Drucker for rectification
Josephine Matsumoto for appreciation
Kate O'Hearn for separation
Lesley Williams for incitation
SilverWood Books for publication

Gentle Reader,

What you have in your hands is a very personal little text. I hope you will understand and forgive when I say that it came into being, not with you in mind but rather that when the words flowed out in succession, I had the feeling that I was writing for myself. In reality the text seemed to write itself, almost automatically, as it were.

Therefore, should you find that what I have written is not to your liking, or should you feel that it contains an approach or ideas with which you do not agree, then please drop it into the nearest waste bin. I shall not be offended in the least, for we each of us have our individual way of trying to understand our place in the universe. Your way is surely quite as valuable as my own.

I say that this text wrote itself and I can find no better way of describing what happened. I was seated at my computer to prepare the outline of a quite different work. Having typed several paragraphs, I discovered that what was appearing on the computer screen seemed to have little connection with what I had intended to write. What was emerging had an independent life and flow that had little to do with me.

Curious to discover what was happening, I let the words run on. After some hours the flow stopped. What had I written? It was not until I printed out the document and read it that I really began to grasp what it was about. Only the beginning was added afterwards to introduce the rest.

On reading through the dialogue I received a considerable surprise. This unexpected and somewhat bewildering exchange made me slightly light-headed, made me chuckle, and at the same time made me reflect profoundly. It took me back to many of those questions I had asked as a child. The adults around me had invariably fobbed me off by replying, "It's a mystery—when you're older, you'll understand". It made me want to show the text to others, to discover whether what I had written was as crazy as the dialogue sometimes appears or whether it made some sort of connected sense to them as well.

Their reaction was also a surprise. They tried to encourage me to share this strange little essay with others—to find a publisher and push it out into the wide world—I, an engineer ten years retired, who had never before published any writing other than a technical paper or report! But what kind of publisher? And for such a bizarre and perhaps inconsequential, writing?

Now that the answer to this question has been found, I hope that you too will chuckle, and then perhaps reflect on the content of this little essay.

Peter St John

Hey God!

What's the time? **Seven o'clock.**
Suppose I'd better get up. **No rush.**
Right, it's my day off: Mary and the kids are with the in-laws.
What's the weather like? **Sunshine.**
Might as well get up then.

Get the
grass cut.

Yes, while it's fine.
Take a shower? **OK.**
This morning I feel like singing. **Why not?**
Right, no one else at home to disturb. Here we go—One man went to mow; **went to mow a meadow.**
One man and his goddog, **went to mow a meadow!**
Goddog? Whatever am I singing? **No matter: it's the right spirit.**
Shave? **Why bother, it's a holiday.**
Might as well, the neighbours could call round. Oh God! I cut myself. **Nothing serious. Bit of toilet paper will fix it.**
Talking to myself? First sign of insanity? **Some breakfast will cure that and a nice cup of tea.**
Where's Mary hidden the tea caddy? **In the cupboard of course.**
Has the paper come? **By the front door.**
Let's have a look: politics on the front page as usual—speculations about the next election. Socialite beauty queen

in sensational sex scandal. Can't they dig up some real news? What's on the telly this evening?

The TV programmes are usually opposite the obituaries.

Macabre juxtaposition. But—What's this? Oh no—not poor old Harry. Oh my God!

Yes. Sad for his family.

What *is* this? Not only talking to myself but giving the answers as well? Still, seeing that death notice in the paper about Harry is a shock. When's the funeral?

Thursday.

Oh God, I've got an important appointment!

Can't you put it off?

Suppose I'll have to. God—am I *hearing* voices now? Second stage of madness? Well, Harry's death is a terrible shock. Perhaps it's Harry talking. That you Harry?

Not Harry—it's me. Or should I say "I"?

Who's I? I mean who *are* you?

I Am.

Who?

I Am. You know—God. "I Am" is my name—that is to say, one of them.

Oh God. I *am* going crazy. I know—it's a spoof!

No spoof.

Got it—
I'm on
candid camera!

Candid perhaps and in camera but not on it. I told you—I'm God!

Now I've got it—I'm being bugged by some Jesus freak.

I've been given quite a few names over the ages but never before "Jesus Freak". You can call me that if you like but I'm usually known as God. It's short—easy to remember.

Is God *really* talking with me? Can't be—it's the news about Harry. I'm really only talking to myself—or it's my imagination. God doesn't exist—does he? Which is it?

Yes.

Yes what?

What you said, and you mean "which" not "what".

OK—which?

Yes—all of them.

It can't be all of them.

Which one do you believe?

You're confusing me. I don't know what to believe. That's why I'm asking you!

But you know the answer. Work it out.

Work it out? I need to sit down for this. Let's see. One: If I'm talking to myself, it's true to the extent I believe I'm talking to myself. But I *am* talking to myself. So that's true. Two: If it's my imagination, it's true to the extent I believe it's my imagination. But I'm getting replies which—if God doesn't exist—must be coming from my imagination. So that seems true too. Three: if God doesn't exist, it's true to the extent I believe God doesn't exist. Do I believe that? Well, if I *really* believed it I wouldn't be going through this reasoning process. So that must be at least partially true. Four: if it's all of them at once, it's true to the extent I believe it's all of them at once. But one is true, two seems to be true and three at least partially true, then—that's it—it's true of all of them at once!

Took you a while, but you got there in the end. Bravo!

I don't believe this. It *can't* be God. I'm going round the bend.

Well, you did call me—several times.

I didn't actually expect an answer.

That'll teach you not to misuse the name of the Lord.

One of the ten commandments?

Number three.[1]

You answered very quickly.

It's not long-distance.

Where are you then?

Everywhere.

Seems like you're inside me.

Inside and outside. I'm everywhere.

You can't be both inside *and* outside.

Why not? You're inside and outside me.

Come again?

Must I repeat it? I'm everywhere. Quite literally everywhere. So outside you is inside me. Conversely, as I'm also inside you, you're on the outside.

Think of a pot full of water immersed in the ocean.

I really *am* ripe for the nut farm—and you're weird.

[1] Exodus 20.7 "You shall not misuse the name of the Lord your God, for the Lord will not hold anyone guiltless who misuses his name."

If you like. But a moment ago you called me "Jesus Freak".

You don't mind me calling you weird?

Why should I mind? I answer to lots of names: Allah, Jehovah, Brahma, The One, Lord, Father, Mother, First Cause, Almighty, Opium-of-the-people, Great Spirit, Supreme Being—even unpronounceable ones like YHWH—lots. What's important is the calling.

But what's your real name?

All of them.

All?

If you like.

Jesus calls you "Father". *Are* you his father?

I'm father to all that exists or ever existed—mother too, for that matter.

And you're inside me? I thought you lived in Heaven.

So I do.

How can you be in Heaven as well as here?

You know that already. I've told you—I'm everywhere.

Even in Hell? The Devil's domain? I don't believe you're in Hell—it's a contradiction.

If you don't believe it, then I'm not in Hell—for you. But if I weren't in Hell too, I wouldn't be God.

You can't have it both ways. If you're in Heaven you can't be in Hell. Which is it?

I tell you—both.

I think that's impossible.

You're right—it is impossible—for you. But I'm everywhere—omnipresent.

I've been to school. I know the word. But I still think it's weird.

So you said.

Then if you are everywhere you must be **in** everything in the whole universe.

It follows.

You *are* everything in fact.

You could put it like that.

How would *you* put it then?

Well, it might be more exact to say that I am in everything and everything is in me. That I am one with everything that exists and the ground of its existence. The total of all that is.

You're not in space. Hah, got you there!

Why not in space?

There's nothing there! It's a complete vacuum. It's absolutely empty.

As you like. But don't the sun's rays traverse this vacuum of yours?

Naturally.

So isn't space full of energy? Some scientists even suggest that it's loaded with virtual particles which come into and out of existence in an unpredictable way. They would say too that solid matter is mainly empty space.

But you can't be in empty space!

What about the energy? I did say "everywhere".

OK. I'll go along with the game, but I still don't fully believe you exist. It's all just in my head. A few simple questions will soon sort it out.

A game? That's good. You've got first move—

It says in the Bible that in the beginning, you made heaven and earth. Was that the Big Bang?

What do you believe?

I don't know *what* to believe. But you were there. You know!

Yes, I am there .

Am there? You mean *was* there.

I know what I said. You am too!

I am?

Yes you am.

What's this weird language we're talking?

It's English, what language would you prefer? I know them all.

Don't brag—and let's stick to English. But please use correct tenses.

I don't need to brag. I'm God, eternal God. Things come out a bit differently depending on when you are as well as where you are. I'm using the present tense for what to you is the past, to help clarify what otherwise may be hard to grasp. For me everything past is also now. It's not for nothing that one of my names is "I Am".

I get the message. But you seem to be implying that I too was present at the beginning.

Well, if I am at that moment, necessarily you are at that moment, too.

If you say so, but I don't remember it.

You have to remember in the right way.

I don't know what you mean. But leave that for now—don't think I won't come back to it.

OK. It's still your move.

For now, I want to know whether the Big Bang was the beginning of everything.

But you know the answer already.

Oh, we've already been round that one. You ask "what do you believe?" I reply, "I don't know", and then you say—

You want me to tell you what to believe? Is that it?

That's it—so tell me.

And take much of the pleasure out of life?

What life?

Eternal life of course, what other life is there?

I'll risk it. Tell me.

You won't like it.

Try me.

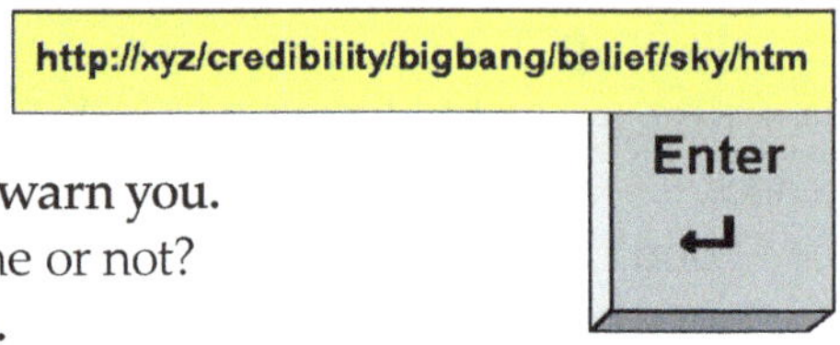

Don't say I didn't warn you.

Are you going to tell me or not?

Suppose I say yes.

Yes what?

The Big Bang was the beginning of everything.

Then what existed *before* the Big Bang?

I told you, you wouldn't like it.

But there must have been *something*.

Not if it was the beginning of everything. By definition there was nothing before that.

That's incomprehensible.

I warned you.

Is it true?

What do you believe?

No need to go round *that* again. But you're God. You must know.

Sorry to disappoint you. If the Big Bang was the beginning of everything, it was the beginning of me too. Your move.

Everybody says you're the creator of everything but that you're not part of creation.

You're somewhere "out there".

In that case you would have been around *before* the Big Bang. Is *that* true?

Everybody says? Look, let's make a deal: You explain what "creator" means and I'll tell you if it's true.

It's a deal: "Creator" means—just a moment I'll find a dictionary.

No hurry, take time—we've got all eternity.

Perhaps *you* have, but today's *my* day off. Where's the dictionary? Here we are: Webster's Third New International. Will that do?

Any dictionary you like. Webster's will do nicely: a reputable work. The result is much the same whichever dictionary you use.

You sound very sure of yourself.

You forget who I am.

Who you *say* you are, but *this* time, I believe *I'm* right.

You believe? That's hitting a bit low. Never mind. Your explanation please?

I quote, "Creator: One that creates, produces, or constitutes". There you are—You can't be both creator and what you create! So you must have been there before the creation—

To set off
The
Big Bang.

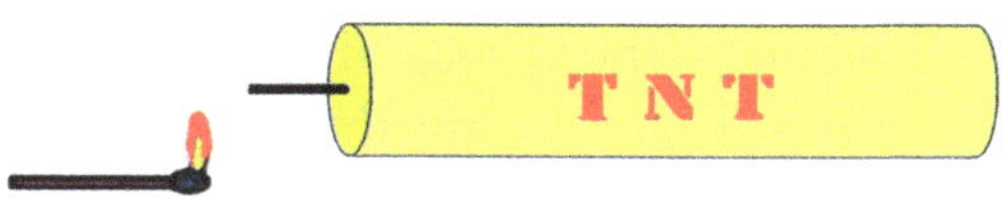

Got you! Your move.

You've got me? Well in a sense you have got me and I've got you. But not in the sense of our deal. Our deal was that you explain what creator means, not give a definition.

But the definition *is* the explanation.

Let's take this step by step. You observe the universe in its immensity and you say to yourself, this didn't happen by itself; it must have been made—created. But I ask you—what is the universe made of?

Why rocks and gases and plasma, and living things and energy and—

That'll do to be going on with. And where did all this matter, and/or energy, all these living things, come from?

You created them.

Out of what?

You just created them.

You mean, you think that there I am, all alone. Just me, nothing else at all—there is not even any time? And then the magic word, abracadabra—

**Suddenly—
Everything
that exists
is there?**

Something like that. Why not? Like a poet creates a poem.

Oh! That's nice. I like that. The whole cosmos an ongoing poem! But is the poem, the poet?

Of course not: the poem is his thought.

So, after I'd said the magic poetic word, "abracadabra" —bang—there was my thought? In that case you too are part of my thought. That's why I suggested that you were present also at the moment of the Big Bang.

But *I'm* not a thought,

I'm solid!

What you'd call "solid thinking", eh? You should ask a cosmic ray or a neutrino about that. They'd tell you that you're so little solid, they'd pass right through you and not even notice you're there!

That's ridiculous. You can't converse with neutrinos!

Can't I though? I've already said that I know every language. There are even some human scientists who are beginning to understand neutrinos. Admittedly, neutrinos don't have much to say. Even assemblies of particles, atoms and molecules, aren't very communicative. But when it comes to viruses and cells, there's just no stopping them.

You're having me on. Nobody can communicate with cells and viruses. That's just a silly fancy.

No body perhaps. Although I suggest that there's a great deal of communication going on right this instant between the cells of your body. And what's a "fancy" but a rather poetic thought? You keep forgetting, I'm omniscient. How do you think I know what's going on? I'm talking with you aren't I?

But I'm not a cell, nor a virus—they're microscopic!

Right—compared with the immensity of the cosmos—

You're even smaller!

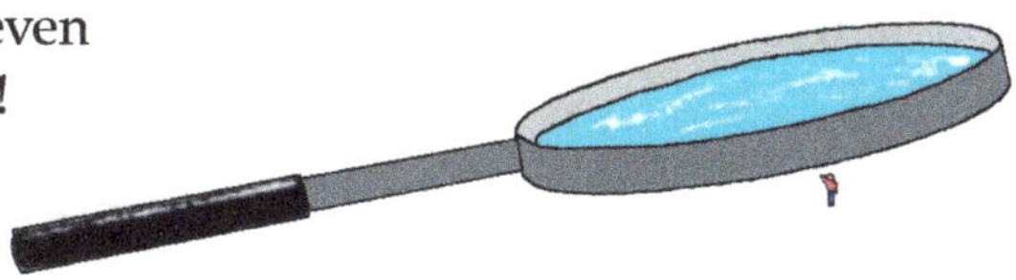

No need to be insulting.

No insult. Merely a fact. Your move—

You said, that before the Big Bang, you were all alone—nothing else at all, not even time.

I didn't say that—I suggested you thought it.

But if time didn't exist before the Big Bang, and you are in an eternal now, then there never *was* a beginning. Like a circle has no beginning. Any beginning would have to be quite arbitrary.

Does that make sense to you?

Can you grasp it?

Not really—but come to think of it, I too am living in the present. At least not in the past, I hope, nor in the future for that matter. Perhaps that's why the idea of continuous creation *feels* somehow satisfying.

Just one Big Bang after another, so to speak?

It's you who say it this time! Your move.

In that case, each Big Bang would have to be followed eventually by an implosion, a Big Crunch. Wouldn't everything be destroyed?

You're asking *me*!

We're playing this game together, aren't we—so what do you think?

I think that, even supposing the universe has cycles of that kind, nothing would be destroyed, because you'd still exist, and you could create new and even better universes.

Don't tell anyone, but perhaps that's more or less how it is. Perhaps some of my latest projects are already launched.

Black holes?

Super-novae?

Shhhh.

Is heaven one of your projects?

That's not what the ancients thought. They believed heaven was my home in the vault of the sky. But let's be modern. Your move.

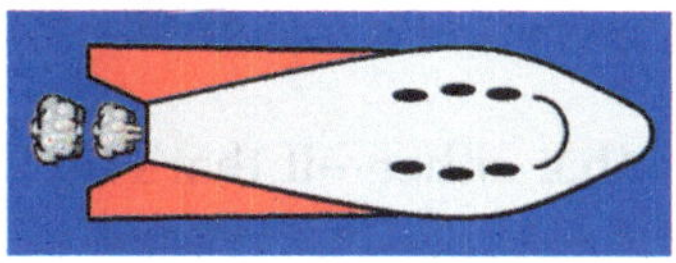

Hey God, you still here?

Of course I'm here. I'm omnipresent, aren't I?

Suppose I believed you weren't omnipresent? What would happen?

Nothing much, except that you would find it hard to get in touch with me.

Suppose everybody in the whole world believed you weren't omnipresent?

It would be even harder. There would still be the rest of the universe however.

But suppose that there was some place where you weren't?

Then I wouldn't be God, would I?

How come?

Well in your hypothetical place where I wasn't, I wouldn't know what was happening, so I wouldn't be omniscient, neither would I be omnipotent, because if I didn't know what was happening, I couldn't do anything about it.

Then who *would* be God?

Only that god would know—no good asking me.

You don't seem to mind me talking with you like this.

Why should I mind?

Well, in religious places,
those in charge
wear fancy clothes,
put on serious faces
and address you with
thees and thous.

I don't mind that either—if that's what they believe is necessary. You too can use the familiar form if you feel more comfortable that way.

Thou is old fashioned.

OK then let's continue to be modern.

Seems to me you'll accept just about anything.

That's what it is to be God.

What *wouldn't* you accept?

Accept isn't quite the word, but I'd miss you if you weren't here.

You, who is one with everything that exists in the whole vast universe, would miss me? How come?

I'm not only omnipresent but omniscient as well. How do you think I could know everything there is to know if you weren't here?

You need *me* in order to know everything? That's hard to believe!

Not really. Reflect an instant and you can work it out for yourself.

Work it out for myself? No—I don't get it. It's a crazy idea. Talking to myself like this I *must* be crazy. I give up.

You give up very easily. Just bear in mind what I said—I am in you—one with you. Also I am omniscient. It follows that your thoughts and experience are essential

for me to know what's happening when and where you are.

You're having me on. You could easily get that from other people around me.

In general, I could indeed, but in the particular, their thoughts and experience wouldn't be exactly the same as yours. I could also get some knowledge from the plants, the animals, the insects around you, but their experiences and thoughts are again, not quite like yours.

Plants, animals, insects—that's absurd!

If you like, but I did say "everywhere", "everything". It goes with being God.

You mean you communicate with insects?

With everything,

as I already said, and with bacteria, viruses, molecules too. Omniscient really does mean knowing every least little thing.

I don't believe it. Religious authorities don't say anything about that.

That's true for the most part. They tend to see mankind at centre stage and this hinders them in following up concepts to their ultimate conclusions. They also focus tightly on a single ancient book. What other books they read, they count of much lesser value.

I've noticed.

Their closeness to a single book tends to veil their eyes.

Because of this they mull over its text and demonstrate their arguments in its light, rather than open their eyes to see me in the book's more profound meaning.

Then they pontificate and preach.

No hard words please! They also care about and help those in need and distress. They represent a powerful moral influence in the world.

As you say.

But whether you, as a lone individual, believe that I communicate or not with all that is, makes but small difference on the cosmic scale. As an omniscient God, it's an essential part of what I am.

You mean you don't *care* what I believe?

Of course I care. It makes a difference to me. Don't you care what your friends think of you?

What I think and believe make a difference to you?

Isn't it obvious? Reflect an instant. I said everywhere, everything. That includes you.

But my thoughts?

Particularly your thoughts, because they are wholly yours! We're agreed that the whole cosmos is like a great thought. It contains the thoughts, rather is the thoughts, together with the consequent beliefs and actions, of everything that ever existed. That includes your thoughts, beliefs and actions of course. So your contribution makes a difference, it changes things.

That's absolutely crazy! The Christian Church says that you are eternal and unchanging. It's still your move.

Why do you think Galileo, Copernicus, Darwin and many other scientists and philosophers were so unpopular with the Church? Wasn't it because their vision took the Earth and man from centre stage, and introduced movement and change?

I don't contest it. But how can what I think change that which is unchanging?

Well, the Church might be on the right track with "eternal" but it seems to have overlooked that everything is in the process of change.

Look at your fingernails!

What have my fingernails got to do with it? Are they dirty?

Are they the fingernails you were born with?

Of course they are!

Are you certain?

Oh. I get it. They're the same but not the *very* same. But that *everything* changes—even you? That change is one of your attributes?

It's like a rug that slips—
a very upsetting notion.

Keep your balance—evolution isn't necessarily revolution. The Church calls me a "living God" but hasn't fully followed through with the implications. Consider your fingernails. Now what do you think? Your move.

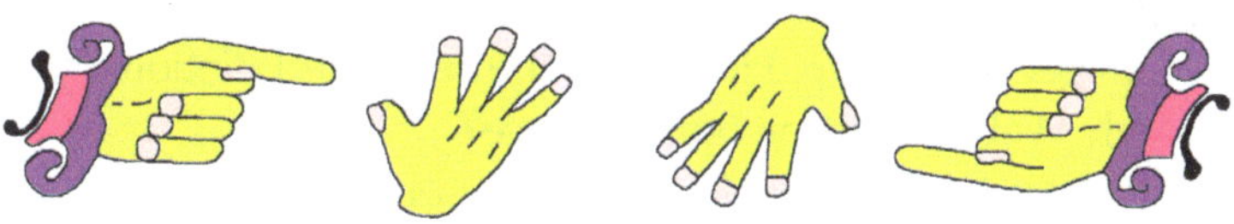

I'm not sure *what* to think. I don't know. You claim to know all there is to know—so *tell* me.

I don't claim anything. I am. In any case if I told you everything, it would spoil our game.

Our game? I don't follow.

The creative and imaginative game of life. Isn't it interesting to live, to construct things and situations, to work out problems?

Depends—often it's pretty miserable hard work. But yes, it *can* be interesting, even enjoyable. But *our* game? You're already omnipotent and omniscient, so how can it be interesting for you, let alone a game?

You're not playing very hard. Consider, I change. Evolve. Eternal change if you like. I know everything there is to know in what you call the here and now. But since the universe is my creative thought, together with the thoughts, beliefs and actions of everything that ever existed, and for sure, in considerable measure predictable, there's still plenty of room for uncertainty.

You mean that if it's interesting and enjoyable for me to work at uncertainty—

Then it is for me too. Your move.

There are things you are uncertain of? Things you don't know? You mean, after all you've said, that you're not *really* omniscient? That you don't know the future? That you have to work at uncertainty?

Why are you so scandalised? You already know the answer to your questions.

I certainly do not!

If you believe so emphatically that you don't, then let us get some help. How does the respected dictionary of Mr Webster define omniscience?

Let's see: Om—omega—omnibus—omnificent—here we are, omniscient: "Having infinite awareness, understanding and insight; knowing all things; infinitely wise." There you are. It means knowing all things! Your move.

That's exactly right. Knowing all things—that are. Infinite awareness of and insight into what exists, including the past which, for me exists eternally. It

doesn't say knowing all things which will be—which have yet to exist. Isn't it your birthday in three weeks?

Yes, so?

Having a party?

Yes, outside, if the weather's fine—and so?

I may be able to help with the weather forecast, I'm quite experienced at projecting forward from the present. Where's the party?

In principle, here but my sister wants to give me a surprise party at her place. I'm not supposed to know.

There seems to be some doubt?

Well, her husband is hoping for a promotion. In that case they will have to move house, and she won't be able to give the party.

Do you think your brother-in-law will get the promotion?

I know he's highly thought of, but competition is stiff. The interviews are still going on. There may be a decision next week. If everything happens at the last minute, he'll need a hand with the removals. Nothing has yet been decided. I need to be free, if necessary, to forget about a party and just celebrate quietly with a family dinner. We can have a party later.

So you're uncertain whether there'll be party or not on your birthday. You're working on it because it depends not only on your decision but on quite a lot of other people as well.

Nothing is yet fixed.

As you say. And yet for me it already is fixed?

I never said that.

Correct—but you were scandalised to think that I don't know the future.

But the decisions haven't yet been made.

As you say—and you need to be free. Are you free?

Relatively free. There are many constraints.

I know what you mean.

Like not knowing the future?

Amongst others. It would be nice to have more time, more money.

Do you feel free; happy?

Sometimes, but what's that to you?

I'm one with you remember. What you feel, necessarily I feel too. What you experience, I too experience. When you're happy so am I.

This is wild! Now I know for sure all this is *only* my imagination. Did I say "only"! But I intend to keep playing and see where it leads. Hey God! Even if *I'm* happy, what about all those who are unhappy. The happiness and the unhappiness cancel out. Your move.

Not so. I didn't say I was the average of everything that is. I said the total.

I don't get it. Mathematics isn't my forte.

Pity about the mathematics, it's a fun subject, and a good

one for finding out more about me.

No kidding?

No kidding. Look at it this way. Two people paint a fence from opposite ends; one with black paint, the other with white.

What colour will the fence be when they meet—black, white or perhaps, grey?

Black and white of course.

You've got it!

But suppose I *believe* the fence to be grey?

To the extent that you really believe the fence is grey, it is grey—for you.

For you too?

For me too—to the extent, and only to the extent, that you believe it to be grey. I am the total of all that is, all activity, all belief, all thought. Now do you see how your thoughts and what you believe make a difference?

Is that the absolute truth?

What's the "absolute" truth?

I thought you are.

Think again. I'm neither absolute truth, nor the arbiter of absolute truth. An absolute is not the total of anything.

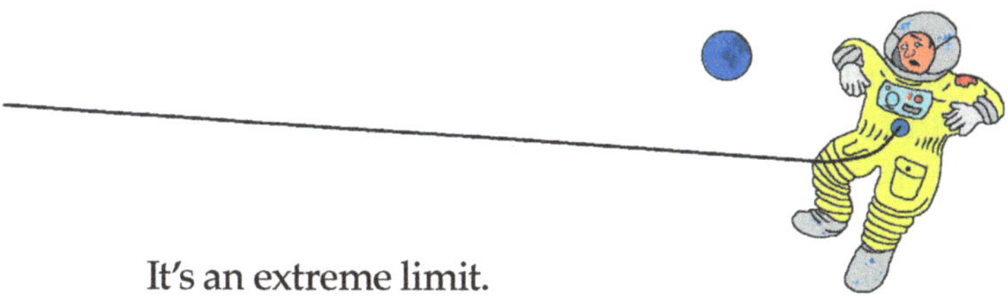

It's an extreme limit.

But something is either true or not true.

Is the fence either black or white? Is nobody using coloured paint?

Nobody writing pertinent or even impertinent graffiti?

I don't believe all this.

Then it isn't true—for you.

I mean that this is happening.

I know what you mean. Your move.

GRAFFITTI+I AM&I AM&I AM!

Listen.

I'm listening.

Suppose *everybody* believes the same thing. For example, in the time of Buddha, of Jesus, everyone believed the Earth to be the centre of the universe and that the sun the moon, the heavens revolved around it.

Many also believed it was flat.

Some still do! But according to you, if *everyone* believed the Earth to be the centre of the universe, then that would be true. But it's not true and it wasn't true then, either. Your move.

You're overlooking something important.

What's that?

It might have been true for all the people of the time, but not for the Earth. It takes a lot of people to outweigh the Earth.

This gets wilder and wilder. The Earth doesn't have beliefs!

Whether or not the Earth has beliefs is not the point.

Are you flat like a pancake?

Of course not!

How do you know?

I just know.

You're sure it's not a belief?

I know.

So does the Earth know.

That it is round?

And that it goes around the sun.

But the Earth isn't conscious, how can it "know" anything?

You believe the Earth isn't conscious. So, for you at any rate—it isn't. But the Earth goes round the sun doesn't it? How does it know to go around the sun? Your move.

Why ask me? I'm not a physicist or an astronomer—oh, all right—it's a balance of forces—gravity and centrifugal force. The Earth doesn't have to be conscious to do what it does.

Perhaps not, but tell me, are you part of the Earth?

Yes.

Your family?

Obviously.

Your pets?

Of course.

They are conscious?

Naturally.

The daisies in your garden are part of the Earth?

Where is this leading?

Are they conscious?

Not that I know.

They know to close at night to protect their pollen from the dew.

They close at night—so?

Are they conscious?

To that extent, yes.

And if your shadow falls on a daisy, does it close?

So it's aware of me after a while—so what?

When you catch influenza—is the 'flu virus conscious?

You mean—is it conscious enough to know to multiply inside me?

You're catching on. Are you conscious, or if you like, aware, of all these beings? Are these beings aware of you?

Put like that, I suppose I have to answer yes.

Put like that, could you not admit, at least the possibility, that the Earth is also aware, or conscious?

I admit the possibility—just.

Just as well, for if the Earth were not sufficiently "aware" of the sun to respond to it, it would fly off into space.

I would explain it differently. More scientifically.

How then?

According to Newton's laws of motion.

Who's laws?

Isaac Newton was the first to set out *your* laws in useable form.

Thank you. And my compliments to Isaac.

According to *those* laws the Earth has a tendency to move in a straight line. However, the Earth is acted upon by a force, the resultant of the Earth's and the sun's gravitational fields, which is inversely proportional to the square of the distance separating them. This gravitational force is equal and opposite to that produced by the product of the Earth's rate of change of motion and its mass, such that the Earth is constrained to move in an ellipse around the sun which is located at one of the foci.

An impressive description.
And the explanation?

That *is* the explanation.

What then is gravitational force?

It seems I can't win, probably because I'm still in bed and dreaming. I intend to go on with the game, anyway, even at the risk of *completely* losing my marbles.

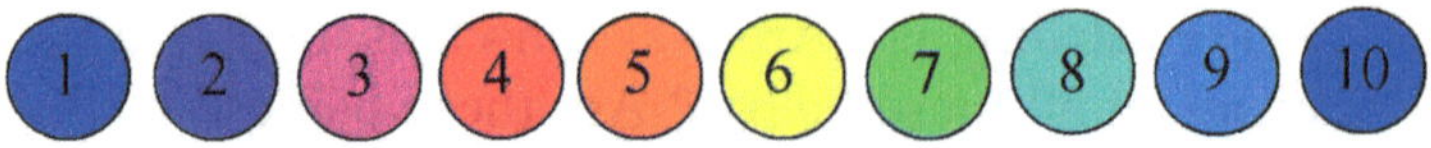

Good. Count your marbles, because it's still your move.

You implied earlier, when speaking of holy books, that if only people would really open their eyes and look, they *could* see you? Your move.

Yes, they could see me—and so?

Everyone says you're invisible. Or that if someone sees you that person will die.

They're entitled to their opinions. But it's not altogether false either.

In that case, why do you suggest that people could see you?

You already know the answer to that.

What? That it's true to the extent that it is believed? Could I see you?

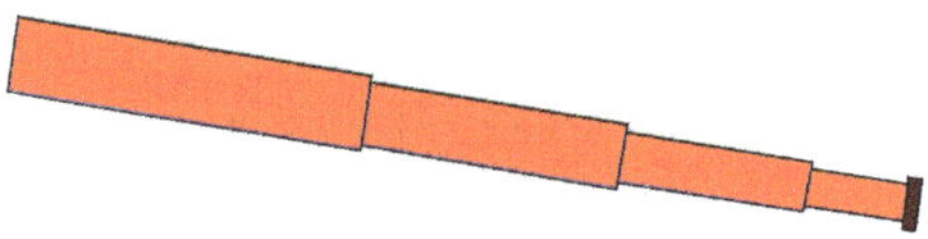

Why don't you look?

I am looking—I see a newspaper lying on a table.

Yes. Look some more.

I still see the newspaper, a table, a television set, a lamp, part of a wall—

Keep looking—really hard.

It's no good, I still don't see you.

You haven't been listening hard enough either. Where am I?

Oh I get it. You're everywhere, one with everything.

Now do you see me?

OK, But I want to *really* see you. As you really are.

You do? What do you expect to see? An old man with a long beard? A splendidly dressed king on a golden throne? A huge thunderstorm? A beautiful Greek goddess? A blinding light? The moon? The sun?

OK, OK, No need to go on. You've made your point—but you implied we were friends.

Aren't we?

Then don't gloat. You knew my answer even before I asked.

True—and so did you, but you didn't realize you knew. So I wasn't really gloating. But aren't friends allowed to gloat a little sometimes, as a sign of affection?

Yes. But you're God.

Does that prevent me from being your friend?

No, but it's not what I expected from God.

Haven't you heard that I'm a loving God?

Of course, but well, you know—forgive me, but—I rather thought that was hardly anything more than a few pretty words.

And now?

Not so much. Even so—

Yes?

If you're so loving—

How come there are so many bad things around?

If you're the total of all that is, then you're the bad things too. Isn't that logical?

That's so. But consider. Who decides what's good and what's bad?

Isn't that your job?

In a certain sense the very idea of my existence provides an ethical background, but in detail, it all depends on thought and belief, on place and time. Remember, I am the total of what is. Like the fence. Black when black paint is used, white when it's white, and grey when it's grey.

I think you're avoiding the issue.

If that's what you think, then that's the truth—for you.

Not for you?

To the extent—

OK, OK—to the extent that I believe it. But *every one* believes it's your job to say what's right and what's wrong, reward the righteous and punish the wrong-doers.

Everyone? Have you consulted everyone? Have you been around to each of the billion million planets in the universe to take a poll?

I mean on Earth.

No need to get heated. I know you mean on Earth. But even on Earth how many are using white paint, how many black and how many are not painting at all?

That's all very well, but surely you don't approve the crimes of great criminals—Hitler for example?

I don't condone crime.

You condemn him then?

I don't condemn Adolf either. I don't judge him at all.

But the Old Testament[2] says you are the great judge who will judge all men.

The writers of the Old Testament are entitled to their opinions.

It isn't true?

Yes it's true—

I know—to the extent that it is believed to be true. Don't you care?

About Hitler? Of course I care. I'm one with him too.

One with Hitler! Impossible! You—a Nazi! Trying to exterminate a whole people and millions of others besides!

I understand how you feel, and to that extent I feel with you. But I am God of the whole universe, not just of some alliance of self-defined "God fearing" people. To the extent of their belief in their own definition, I am what I am. If they feared me more, they'd be less free with the use of my name.

[2] Psalms. 7:8 "Let the Lord judge the peoples. Judge me, O Lord, according to my righteousness, according to my integrity, O Most High."

Hitler deserves to go to Hell!

You're hasty with your judgments! Better not to judge at all. But as for Hell, then he is there—if that's what he too believes.

You surely wouldn't have him in Heaven?!

Why not? He'd find there a lot of people he's wronged.

I think he'd very soon want to go somewhere else!

I see you have a sense of humour.

And why not? If I'm the total of all that is, necessarily I have a sense of humour.

It doesn't seem right to me that you should make jokes.

That's your opinion. I hear and appreciate millions of jokes every day.

You're not serious. There's a lot of wickedness in the world. Why don't you do something about it?

About wickedness as you see it? Well, I am serious too. Remember—black paint, white paint. And I am involved, profoundly involved, in everything. But the kinds of things you're talking about are in your domain.

You could stamp out terrorists!

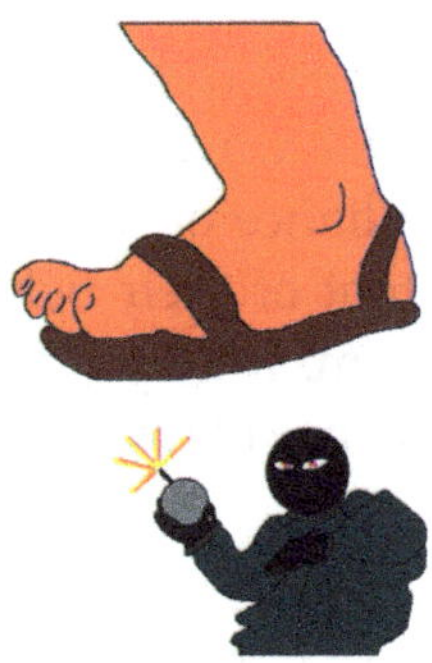

Could I? I'm one with each of them too. Like I said—your domain.

You mean you *won't* help? I thought you could do anything.

Not "anything"—any old thing at all. But all things are possible with me.[3] I'm God—not the US Marine Corps.

You're in the US Marine Corps aren't you?

Well, not as a recruit, but I understand what you mean.

So why don't you just send them over where they're needed and get rid of terrorism?

And get a medal from the President?

The Americans have already kindly given me a mention on their bank notes. On the other hand, many of those opposed to the USA also claim to act in my name. Moses had a point with his commandment number three. Dispatching the Marines is the President's job, not mine.

You could show them where to go and what to do.

I help gladly—when asked.

You could give orders to the President.—

Look—do I push you around?

[3] Matthew 19:26: "With man this is impossible, but with God all things are possible."

No.

Why not?

You're a loving God and we're friends.

So why should I push the President of the United States around, or the Marines, or any other body or anything?

Your move.

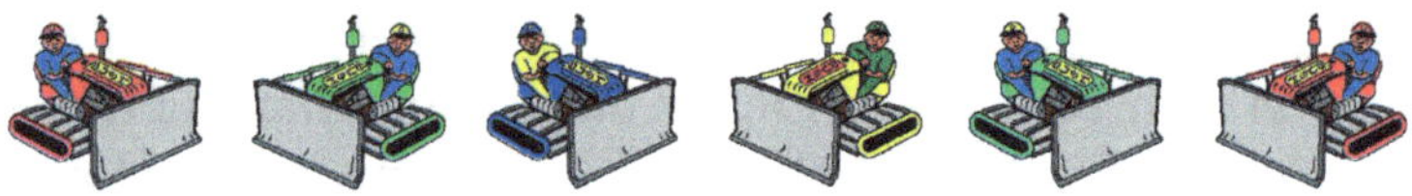

You say you're omnipotent, but I know one thing you can't do—sleep. You have to stay awake all the time, or you wouldn't know what was going on. If you slept, you wouldn't be omniscient. Some say you're asleep now, even dead!

Why do they say that?

I think they're expecting some dramatic intervention on your part to miraculously make the world more to their liking.

Like parting the Red Sea so Moses and the Israelites could cross?

Something like that.

Moses had courage, charisma, a "magic" staff, detailed knowledge of the region and a good biographer.

You mean you had nothing to do with it?

I mean nothing of the kind. It was a dramatic, historic event described in a very striking way. But it certainly didn't solve all Moses' problems. I was there and not sleeping.

I guess those who believe you're asleep or dead had hoped

you'd arrange things for their benefit so that the goodies win and the baddies lose. Like the hero in a western.

And, like the hero, they decide who's good and who's bad. They, of course, are the goodies. Suppose that in their judgment they consider you bad because you seem to be making fun of me? Mocking God is blasphemy. Commandment number three again.

But I'm *not* breaking that commandment.

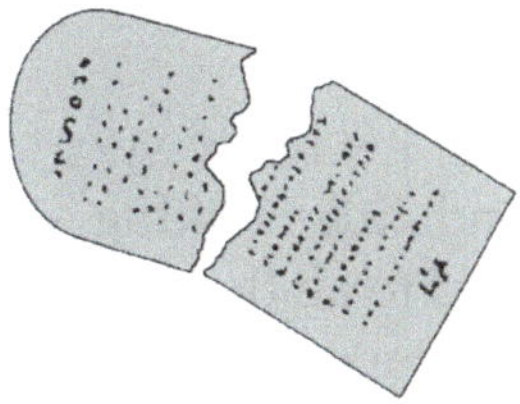

We're friends.

I know that. But they may not see it the same way.

So you stay awake to be on guard?

That's not it. But, in a way, you're right about me sleeping.

You mean—how can you be omniscient and also sleep, unless every sentient being sleeps at the same time that you do? Even then they would have not to dream—not to breathe even.

Indeed. Everything would have to stop.

It's unimaginable! Couldn't you create another universe, just for sleeping?

Every seventh day? Thank you for the compassionate, reposeful thought. But the solution is easier than creating universes. You see, if I didn't rest, as written in Genesis, there'd be no flow of time.

Whaat! Now I've heard it all! I need more than a *day* off—

I need
A long
holiday!

Relax. It's really very simple. How do you think I can spend time talking with you and at the same time attend to all the other countless billions of things going on in the universe?

Really, I've never thought about that. I've no idea.

So think about it now. You divide your 24 hour day roughly into three parts: eight hours work, eight hours for other activities, eight hours sleep.

What's the length of my day?

Your day? Your *day*? You don't have a day, or rather, it's eternity—infinitely long.

Right. And if I divide it into three parts like you, how long is each part?

I told you already that maths is not my forte, but to that, I know the answer—infinity divided by three equals infinity. It is, indeed, quite logical.

And if I divide by a million, billion, billion?

The answer is still infinity.

So I have infinite time for every separate little thing in the universe, including you.

But time—the flow of time—what's your resting got to do with that?

How do you experience the flow of time?

Not easy to answer, but it's like now, followed by now, followed by now, in an extremely rapid sequence—like a continuous flow.

How long is the separation between each instant of now? What's between each instant?

If such separations exist, they are so short they can't be detected. Impossible to say.

Impossible? I suggest they are infinitely long—my personal moments of eternity. My rest periods!

What fantasy. My imagination is working overtime! And completely paradoxical! After that I need a rest. Suppose we take a break—a cup of tea?

Good idea. Let's go into the kitchen.

You're all powerful. Why don't *you* bring me a cup of tea here?

You wouldn't like it.

Don't you know how to make a cup of tea? I thought you knew everything?

I make excellent tea.

So why not bring me a cup here?

You wouldn't like it.

The tea?

The consequences.

Never mind that—I'm thirsty.

Just bring
the tea
please—

So how was the tea?

But I haven't had it yet.

Indeed you have, and declared it excellent!

Nonsense!

I said you wouldn't like it.

What do you mean?

I create for you a universe in which it is possible for me to bring you a cup of tea. You drink it. Declare it excellent—

And then?

And then you want me to do the washing up! So, I create another universe in which I can do the washing up.

What happened to the first universe?

You didn't specify what should happen after the cup of tea—and in any case, if my creation is capable if ordering me around, what happens to my omnipotence? The universe quickly became chaotically unstable. The end was spectacular.

The end?

Of course—the Big Crunch.

You're having me on. None of this happened. It isn't possible.

With me, all things are possible.

Then how come I remember nothing of it? I was there wasn't I?

You were there. But the "you" created for that universe existed in another space-time and disappeared in its Big Crunch. It doesn't exist now. How then could the "you" in this space-time have any memory of the "you" in that space-time?

How come *you* remember then?

Before that Universe's Big Bang, I am.

Well what about the second universe—the one where you do the washing up?

Same story—Big Crunch. I said you wouldn't like it. Still want me to bring you a cup of tea?

Let's go into the kitchen.

I'll put the kettle on—

You make a really good cup of tea.

Thank you, but how do you know?

Well, you drank it, didn't you?

I drank it, not you.

That's right.

You mean—you drank my tea too?

Naturally—I drink millions of cups all the time. I've drunk a goodly number just while we've been talking. That's the reason I am able to make a fully informed comparison between your tea and others. Your tea was delicious.

That doesn't make sense!

What, about the quality of your tea?

No—the millions of cups.

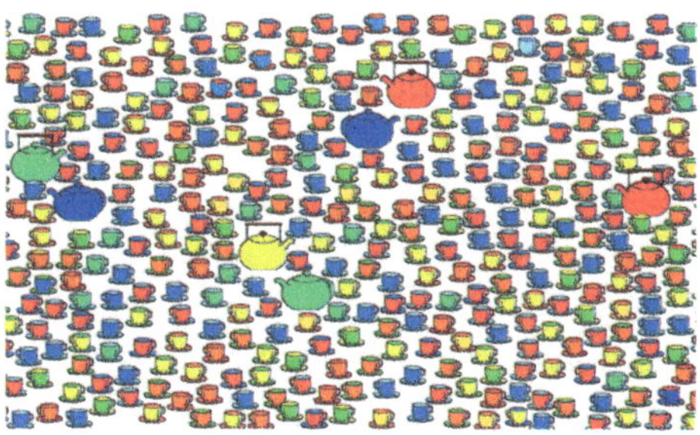

It doesn't make sense? Think about it. How can I be omnipresent, not to say omniscient, and not drink millions of cups of tea?

That's crazy!

Isn't it, but it follows, logically.

I don't believe it.

Then the universe is crazy—for you.

I didn't say that!

Forgive me, I distinctly heard the word "believe".

I meant the cups of tea idea, and those two universes.

Didn't you agree that I am creator? What makes you think I created just once and then went into retirement? Do poets write only one poem?

You mean you really *did* create those two universes?

I create a great many. Most of them don't work too well, so I do what other poets do.

That is?

Big Crunch.

I don't believe it.

As you please. But I ask you—am I creator or am I not creator? It seems you're not willing to follow up the consequences of your belief. If you believe something—like the statements in a creed—then it's true; at least for you.

You mean, I had better be careful what I believe?

Bang on,
and I do mean
Bang!

But how do I know what to believe and what not to believe?

Use your equipment!

My equipment? What equipment?

I create a universe in which there are well-equipped beings, able to share with me in the pleasure of creative activity, and this one doesn't even realize he's equipped for it. Sometimes I feel another Big Crunch coming on.

No need to get huffy, I only asked a simple question.

Exactly, so simple, you can answer it for yourself.

You mean—my body, my hands, my head?

You're on the right track. Keep going.

There isn't any more—oh—and my heart!

Keep going—

Imagination?

Any more?

Uh—critical faculty, intuition—

You could also consult me, after all, we're in this together.

You mean—meditation, inspiration, prayer?

Something like that. But be careful what you pray for. You're likely to receive it—remember the cup of tea!

You could also use some of your tools.

Tools?

Tools—you know, disciplines like physics, astronomy, philosophy, psychology, theology, mathematics. All knowledge in fact. The sorts of things you find in books as well as elsewhere. Things like that.

Thought you didn't like books—when you spoke of reading just a single book—

You misunderstood me.

Books
are
wonderful

They are thoughts made manifest. Creative acts shared with others. Not only that—most of them are about me—even if I'm only in the wings, so to speak.

Oh—the Bible, the Koran, the Brahma-Sutra!

**Amongst
many
others.**

What about those books that say you don't exist?

Those in particular. They're about me too. The argument is sometimes quite ingenious.

Don't you want to ban them? How about the "naughty" books?

You mean those on the Vatican's Index?

It wasn't exactly what I had in mind, but—

I know it wasn't, but I trust you would use your tools and equipment to decide what is worthwhile and what isn't. If you don't also know the "naughty" books, how can you make well-informed choices?

But what about children and fragile people?

Helping others to select books or other information, appropriate to their stage of development, is not censorship.

But it implies restrictions.

Certain rules may be judicious.

You would make rules then?

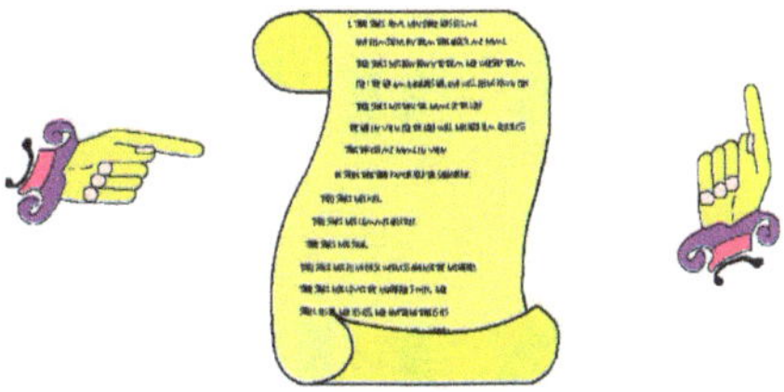

I don't make rules, I am. I leave the rule-making to you. Aren't we in this together?

But Moses on Mount Sinai—you gave him the ten commandments.

You want to take away from Moses the honour that is his due? I gave him nothing more than advice. I suggested that he would do well with something positive. He considered it, but decided his punchy list of prohibitions was best in the circumstances. The commandments are his.

You mean they don't apply any more?

I don't mean anything of the kind. That's for you to decide.

You mean you won't help?

I do help. What about the Buddha, what about Jesus of Nazareth?

I thought you *are* Jesus.

Well, if you believe I am, then I am!

And if not?

Then not.

You can't simultaneously be Jesus and not Jesus.

Why not? An electron can be simultaneously wave and particle.

A paradox?

I know, I love a paradox. A paradox can reveal the truth.

Christians believe you're Jesus.

I rather fancy they would say that Jesus is me.

It's the same thing!

SAME THING
=
GNIHT EMAS

Not quite.

Sometimes you can be extremely frustrating.

I know.

So are you going to tell me?

What?

Whether you are Jesus of Nazareth or Jesus of Nazareth is you.

But you've had the answer already.

I have?

It's your move—

What's this about an electron being simultaneously wave and particle?

It's physics.

Oh yes—I remember from school. If you shoot an electron—a particle—at a screen pierced by two small holes and equipped with instruments to detect which hole it goes though, the instruments show it going through both holes at the same time. That is, it seems to be in two places at once!

Not only that—it then produces a diffraction pattern of the kind that a wave creates when it encounters two holes.

It seems impossible.

Yet that's how it is.

I've heard it said that the number of electrons in my body is of the same order as the number of stars in the universe.

So you're a kind of mini-god of your own private universe.

With innumerable paradoxes!

Something like that, but don't let it go to your head.

I know how many electrons there are.

Do you?

Hey God! Can I ask you something?

Why not, ask away.

Where was I before I was born?

But you know the answer already.

If you weren't here I'd say a rude word!

But I'm always here—so say it, if it'll make you feel better. I hear plenty of rude words all the time.

F***! Why can't you ever give a straight answer?

But it was a straight answer. You've just proved it with your expletive.

"F***" is the answer?

I thought you asked where you were before you were born.

And "f***" is the answer?

Isn't it?

Doesn't satisfy **me.**

It doesn't? Ah—well, "love-making" would be more socially acceptable—intercourse more technical. What you really meant to ask was: Where were you before you were conceived?

You *know* what I meant!

My little joke. But if you want clear answers you must ask clear questions. And I repeat—you already know the answer.

I do not.

As you prefer. Let's take it step by step then. What are the possibilities?

The possibilities?

Your hypotheses if you like, as to where you were before you were conceived?

It's my day off—I haven't got the rest of my life to spend going through all the possibilities.

Why not make a start instead of procrastinating. Just for fun.

For fun? OK, you asked for it. Hypothesis number one: I was in the egg of my mother and the sperm of my father which came together at my conception. But that's two things. I'm only one.

Are you? What about all the cells that make up your body? What about all the molecules with their electrons that are in two places at once?

OK, accepting that by some miracle I can be in two places at once—where did my mother's egg and my father's sperm come from?

Again, you already know the answer to that.

From *their* parents?

Like I said. You know already.

I was in my grandparents. Is this *true*?

For the moment we're dealing with hypotheses, not truths. Continue.

My grandparents were in *their* grandparents.

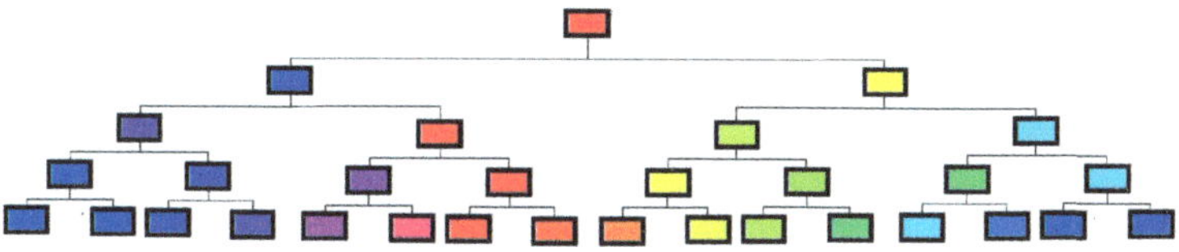

They were in their grandparents and so on and so on, back to the first man and woman. Adam and Eve.

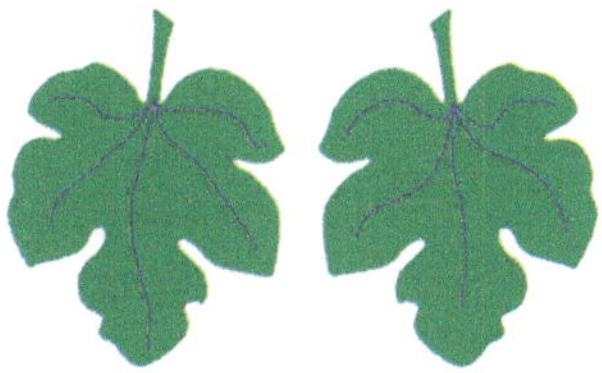

That makes quite a crowd of people.

Right. So you are related, in fact, to everyone who has ever existed. Are you going to stop there?

You created Adam and Eve, in which case, I come from you?

That's one line of reasoning.

I prefer Darwin's theory concerning the evolution of species. The first man and woman had their "non-human" parents. And *they* had parents, and *they* had parents, and *they* had parents—right back to the first living thing.

Is that where you're going to stop? Where did the first living thing on Earth come from?

From the materials around it.

Where else? And where did the materials come from?

From the sun, the stuff planets are made of, space dust—the Big Bang.

And the Big Bang?

That was you too.

I'm related
to everything!

Next hypothesis please.

What is this—kindergarten?

Polite request. I'm interested. Aren't you?

Hypothesis number two: I came into existence at the moment of my conception. Before that I didn't exist at all.

Your private big bang as it were.

**A little bang
for you alone?**

And my parents.

Let's hope so. So you are your own mini-universe. An intriguing hypothesis. Tell me, have you any idea of what existed before the Big Bang?

You did—God.

And before the little bang?

Er—god, with a small "g"? Though that's not part of the hypothesis.

Back to me again?

Perhaps. Because I'm left with a feeling that somehow I did indeed exist before the little bang.

So, if you like, you can put that into your next hypothesis.

Hypothesis number three: I had had a previous existence and was "out there" somewhere, with you say, at the moment of the little bang and took advantage of the event to become the embryo.

Out there?
Out where?

In another dimension, another universe, outside time—or perhaps my last conception was simultaneous with my previous death.

Delayed or immediate reincarnation in other words?

Yes. At any rate, returning from a previous existence.

You mean you could have been Napoleon?

Oh no—not Napoleon. Anyone who thinks they're Napoleon—

Is mad? Napoleon's horse then?

That's even madder.

Napoleon's hat?

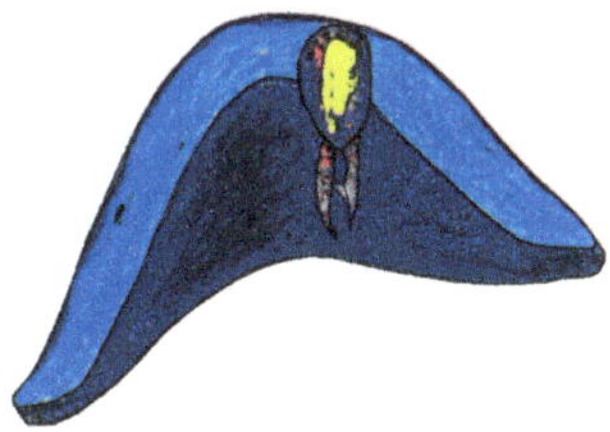

You're making fun of me!

Just testing your hypothesis. Why not Napoleon's hat? What happened to his hat?

Probably in a museum.

All his hats?

Most of them would have completely rotted away by now.

That is to say, incorporated into other matter—to bacterium, to other micro-organism, to worm, to bird. A chicken say. Perhaps the very one you had for lunch yesterday. Napoleon's hat could indeed be part of you now.

Whose hypothesis **is** this? By reincarnation I mean of a previous person.

How did it work before Adam and Eve?

Living beings then.

Before the first living being?

This is mad.

It's your hypothesis!

Before the first living being the question doesn't arise—matter is already matter. It isn't conscious. It is just there from the Big Bang.

So your reincarnation hypothesis ends there. I was rather hoping it would come back to me again. Next hypothesis please.

No—wait a moment—perhaps I *can* bring it back to you.

No need to force it.

It does seem
a bit forced,
but still—

Still?

All living things contain, indeed depend for their reproduction, on the DNA molecule. The molecule is a complex chemical derived from the material around it. Molecules of the sort are even detected in deep space! The material for DNA was created in the Big Bang. So Bingo, we're back to you!

"Bingo" is the magic word then?

I did say it was a bit forced. Fun all the same.

Glad you're enjoying our game. It's still your move.

Now, hypothesis number four: Reincarnation again, but not so much of a person or individual living being, rather of what is essential from previous lives.

The wheel of life? Goes on round and round eternally.

Ever changing, ever the same?
Could be, though that doesn't satisfy me either.
Why not?

It goes
round
and round.

There's revolution but no progress—no evolution. Also the idea that I'm a sort of smorgasbord of previous lives—a bit of this, a bit of that, a bit of the other—is very off-putting. There's no plan nor point to it.
Could it be true?
Not as far as I'm concerned. But those who do believe in it, could get horribly caught-up in the works. Perhaps never escape!
So much for that hypothesis. Any more?
Hypothesis number five: Similar to number four

but with
a sense of
direction.

Bear in mind that your question is "Where was I before I was conceived?"

I haven't forgotten—I mean the question, not previous incarnations. So there I was in the world, going round the wheel of life but at the same time giving it a sense of direction.

Would you still be doing it in this incarnation?

Evidently—that's part of the hypothesis. It's the idea of Karma.

How does it work—this "sense of direction"?

Well, everything that I do, think, believe, has an effect, however small, on what exists, and so—

Wait a moment—haven't we already touched on this?

So we have.

What was the conclusion?

I had better be careful—

What you believe.

That's what I was coming to. Belief, thought, action give everything a sense of direction.

Is everything going in the same direction?

Of course not. What counts is the total.

Of black and white?

Of black and white—*and* colour.

And why can't you remember all the previous incarnations?

Uh—The present me isn't *exactly* the previous "me". Each successive incarnation contributes its modifications. There is also the element of choice. Some people, however, do claim to remember—at least a bit. If I were as you are, I *would* remember—completely.

Omniscient?

Disembodied.

Just testing. Next hypothesis?

I don't think there *are* any more possibilities.

Thought this was going to take the rest of your life?

Oh—I can think of *one* more.

So, let's have it.

Not so fast. I need to work it through—

Hypothesis number one is about a biological mechanism operative since the beginning.

Number two is the one time little creative bang; not fully compatible with number one but not incompatible either.

Number three concerns "complete" reincarnation from a previous life. It's conceivable that number one provides the mechanism for three.

Number four, the wheel of life, is likewise not entirely compatible, but could be made so, depending on how one looks at it.

Number five, the directional wheel of life, also has some incompatibilities with number two. But why should I suppose that there is one answer, and one answer *only*? Much could depend on individual circumstances. So—it *could* be all the hypotheses at once.

Is that the answer?

I believe
it is!

Didn't I say you already knew?

Clever Dick!

**There have
to be some
advantages
to being God.**

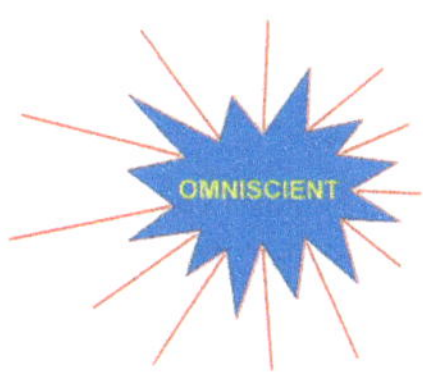

All that leads up to another question.

So, what is it?

Where do
I go when
I die?

Your turn now.

Where would you like to go?

Well, since I've got to know you better, I think I'd rather like to be with you, and with my family and friends.

Thank you—but you're with me now. How would it be different after your death?

I wouldn't have a body.

So—you could zip around easier and see the sights better. Revisit all the past—if that's what you'd like. There are all kinds of possibilities.

Other possibilities? You mean wear wings and play the harp?

If that amuses you. Or you could continue to give a hand in some of my projects, for example. You'd have to be sufficiently qualified of course. Can't have my partners making too much mess. Even so, he who never made a mistake, never made anything.

You're having me on again.

Not convinced about the messes? Just turn on the TV news! I seem to recall that it was you who raised the problem of terrorism. Fortunately, eternal life provides plenty of time for evolution.

What about reincarnation?

If you like.

Are you Buddhist then?

It's not only Buddhists who believe in reincarnation. What about Jesus?

Jesus didn't preach reincarnation.

He used different words.

Like?

Didn't he talk about being reborn to enter the kingdom?

That's not reincarnation!

Isn't it?

But what about your judgement after death?

My judgement? I'm creator, not judge. I'm not eligible to be judge.

Not eligible? How come?

Do you write poetry?

Sometimes.

Good. What do you write about?

Oh things that interest me, things that make me angry, things I love.

Things you love, like your friends?

My friends, my pets. I have a bird I love very much.

Has the bird got a name?

Yes—Mopsy.

Funny sort of name.

Funny sort of bird.

Right, suppose you write a poem about this Mopsy you love. And because of your love, you love your poem also.

And then?

Then you enter your poem in a competition.

With you so far. What then?

You are asked to be judge of the competition.

I can't be judge.

And why not?

I'd be biased in favour of my own poem. I wouldn't be able to judge fairly. And even if I did, nobody would trust my judgement. But you're *not* a poet.

I'm creator, and we already agreed that being creator is like being a poet. Right this instant I'm creating as many poems as you can possibly imagine and then more. About more subjects than you can enumerate, even if you spent the rest of eternity counting. I love every one of them. One of my poems even has your name on it. You still want me to be judge?

Who **will** judge then?

Why judge at all? The point of a poem is to enter into the thought of its author and to savour and enjoy the writing.

But who will decide if I'm to go to heaven or to hell?

What a black and white way of thinking you have!

Well, who told me about the fence being painted?

Touché. I like a bit of spirit,

no pun intended, Jesus has plenty. You—you will judge yourself. In fact, in a sense you're doing it now, even this very moment. Your move.

Well I've heard some strange things today. But this really takes the cake. I can't imagine how it is possible that I am deciding here and now, what's going to happen on my judgement day. Your move—and it had better be good!

What have we been talking about? No, I've not forgotten. I just want to make sure you've been paying attention. Your move.

I've been talking with *you* haven't I? Who wouldn't pay attention when God speaks?

Sure you weren't just talking to yourself?

No, if you really want to know—I'm *not* sure!

Angry eh? A little anger does no harm. Only a little, mind. Jesus is often angry. You believe, however, that perhaps you were also talking partly with me. Not a very powerful belief, but it'll do.

You convinced me you are eternal, omnipotent, omnipresent, and omniscient. Oh—creator and loving. Also that my contribution counts.

Good. And omniscient means?

Kindergarten again?

Something like that. Omniscience please?

It means knowing everything there is to know. Absolutely everything. Everything from the very beginnings of all that is.

That means your beginnings as well.

You mean from my birth?

If I meant "your birth", I would have said so. I meant just what I said. But "from your birth" will do for now.

But you know all that about me *now*. How will it be different after my death?

But you've already said it. You won't have a body.

So—we'll still be friends won't we?

For my part yes. But your body won't be there as a screen between us.

You mean I will be aware of you, not partially, bit by bit, as now, but all at once. Pow! And I will be aware of myself completely from the very beginning, in the same way you already know me. *POW!* Aieee, aieee, aieee, aieee, aieee!

What are all these strange noises? Are we still using English?

It's not funny. I've got to think about it—hard.

Don't do yourself an injury. I'll still be here, same as ever.

Yes, but will I be able to take it? I must really think about this; meditate on it.

Meditation is not a bad idea. Look at the Buddha.

Lots of people think you *are* the Buddha.

We're pretty close—except that his ideas about my existence don't involve belief, in the ordinary sense of the word.

He thinks I'm empty.

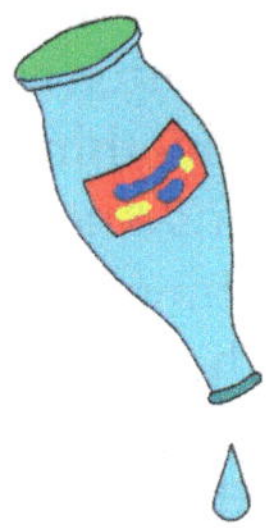

Empty?

Well, his kind of emptiness is rather full.

Another paradox?

Another paradox.

How can you two be so close, when he thinks you're empty?

That's our secret—but why not consult him? Or the Dalai Lama?

I'm asking *you*! What's this notion of emptiness?

You know the answer already—in a way.

If I knew it, would I be asking you?

"'Seek and ye shall find' eh?"[4]

Why do you have to be so enigmatic?

Not as enigmatic as all that—the notion is not easy to grasp.

So, suppose we take it step by step?

OK. Let's try. The idea is based on the realisation that nothing exists independently of itself, but rather in relation to everything else. For example: You have a name. Is your name you?

My name is a word, not me.

So your name is empty.

I get it. My name isn't me. But I'm still me, even if I don't have a name. If I look in the mirror, for instance, I can see myself.

Is that image you?

Of course not.

So it's empty, right? Shut your eyes. Now where are you?

I feel as though I'm in my head.

Is your head you?

Oh I get it. My head is also empty.

That's easy to believe.

That's an insult!

No insult—it's the simple truth—if you're the Buddha.

[4] Luke 11:9 "Ask and it will be given to you; seek and you will find."

Then, if I'm not in my head, which is "empty", the very *idea* that I'm in my head is also empty.

Keep going.

But the idea of everything, including you, is in my head.

So?

That idea, also, is "empty". Therefore, I'm "empty". *Everything* is "empty".

Like before the Big Bang? I told you, you knew the answer already.

But if I'm "empty", I don't exist!

You've already said, that even without a name, you are still you.

You mean—I *know* I exist?

So there's no need to prove it—like Descartes tried to do, with his famous proposition, "I think, therefore, I am"

"Think"; "I am"?

I AM & I AM & I AM!

Intriguing, isn't it?

Are the thoughts on emptiness, Buddhism?

There's very much more to Buddhism than that. But development of your "Buddha nature" by reflection and meditation, together with the practice of compassion,

are close to the core of it. It's in the Bible too.

Where?

Oh, in lots of places. Try psalm 145 verse 8 or psalm 46 verse 10.

Poetry again?

Yes, very appropriate. What do you read?

"The Lord is gracious and full of compassion", and "Be still, and know that I am God". I'm not fully convinced.

Have it your own way, but what was the Buddha doing when he became enlightened?

He was meditating under a banyan tree. He'd been there a while.

He wasn't rushing around then?

No, he was sitting still.

Right—Just like Jesus often did, when he went into the wilderness or up on a mountain to pray.

Jesus was a Buddhist?!

Is your head really empty?

Not as empty as all that. I know he was a Jew. He just went around teaching people that the majority of the religious laws were "empty".

Which didn't endear him to the religious authorities!

All that's very interesting, but the burning question is—where will I go after my death? I thought you were my friend. You make jokes instead of giving me advice and this is a crisis. Will I be able to take it when I die? How will my fate be decided?

No panic—it won't be as burning as all that. The decision will be made and you'll be able to take it. It happens to millions of people constantly, not to speak of all the other beings that die.

But the decision, the decision. How will it be made and by whom?

As I said, I can't be judge, so the decision is up to you. You carry on as though you'd never ever taken a decision, when in fact you're constantly doing it. If you didn't, nothing would ever change.

You keep on about change but I can't change *myself*.

Is that a decision?

No, a statement of fact.

As you prefer. Sounded rather like a decision to me. Whatever you decide I'll still be here same as ever.

Didn't you say one of your characteristics is "continual change"?

That's what I said—
"same as ever".

Another paradox!

Right.

Can I change I wonder yet still stay the same?

Are you asking me?

Oh go away, this time I'm talking to myself.

I can't go away—I'm omnipresent.

Oh God!

Yes?

Why don't you go away!

You really want me to go away? Really and truly?

Yes.

You wouldn't like it. Remember your little bang.

So?

Microscopic crunch.

Sorry, I was panicking—and thinking of Harry!

It's all right. I understand.

Hey God! Is he OK?

Relax—there's no need to panic. You already know the

answer to your question about Harry, as well as to how you are making the decision now. Incidentally, it's the same for Harry as it is for you.

Oh oh, here we go again.

Yes, here we go again. You were telling me about your birthday party. Your wish to remain free to decide. Cause and effect.

Cause and effect? Did I say that? What's that got to do with it anyway?

Your birthday party seems to depend largely on your brother-in-law's boss. If he promotes your brother-in-law, he will be the cause of a whole chain of events, one of the effects of which is where, when and whether your party will be held.

So?

But if you think the weather will be good next week, and you also believe your brother-in-law will get the promotion, you can decide to have the party early at your place. That will then be the cause of an entirely different set of effects.

You mean my thought, my belief, and my action, influences—

Everything that follows it! It's not pre-ordained. It's part of your Karma.

Of course, within limits, I'm free to choose and decide.

What would make it any different after your death? Why are you so concerned about that?

But Saint Peter's book?

You imagine it's an enormous ledger of your sins and good actions? I thought we had decided to be modern?

You mean he's traded his book for a computerised data base—with all your omniscience in it?

Well, not quite all of it, but you've got the broad idea.

I'm going to make another cup of tea—

I need one after all that. Then I'm going to take my imagination in hand, do some serious thinking and fix all this God stuff.

I thought you said you couldn't change yourself? You've just made, right there, a pile of decisions for change.

Those aren't decisions. They are just—er, just—thinking out loud.

Well, what are decisions then, according to you?

They are big things like deciding to get married, deciding where to live, deciding if I'm going to change my job, deciding to buy a new car, deciding to repaint the house—

Deciding which shirt to put on—?

That's just a fiddling little thought that I make almost automatically every day, not a real decision.

Have it your own way. I would have called it a decision. It changes your appearance at any rate. But isn't a decision which changes your way of thinking a "big" decision?

Why do you always have to win, to be right?

I have neither to win, nor to be right—I am! As partner,

your thoughts, decisions and actions affect me. If you don't like what your imagination is producing—change the subject.

I will—I'm fed up with this game! Where's the newspaper? Something that has nothing whatever to do with God. Stock market, the very thing.

Let's see—All Ordinaries up half a point, IBM slipped two-and-a-half percent, Mercantile Credits holding steady. How are those Neotech shares I bought last week doing? My God, NO!

You called?

I called? Never on your life! I just said—

Thought I heard my name.

I was just reading the stock market news and you'd never believe—

Right—I never believe—I know—

Your Neotech shares have plunged.

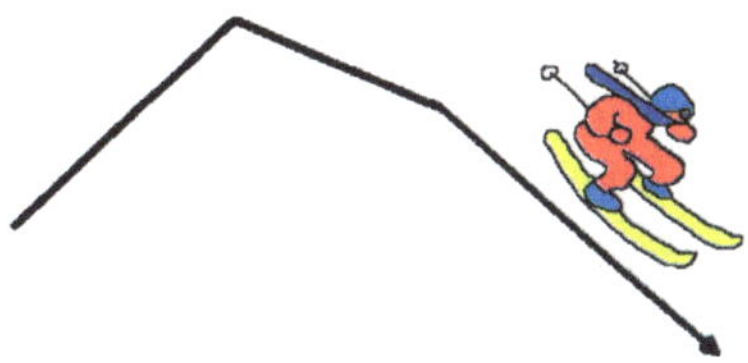

I was reading the paper to get *you* out my head.

You know very well that you can't get me out of your head.

Out of my thoughts then.

Your thoughts are your own.

That's nice. I was beginning to think you owned everything.

I know what you are thinking, of course.

But *my* thoughts belong to *me*, they're my responsibility, and I'm free to make them as I please.

So that's that. Amen, hallelujah! Hard to believe, after all your talk of omnipotence and such.

You don't have to believe me. You can test it for yourself. Just think of something, anything you like, and you'll see.

OK, a limerick:

Non ead too grum bullorg reeve
The troo this watchoob eleeve.
Iffit's why tor it's blak
Orcul ors doughnut lak,
The toe tals the sumso dount peeve.

You're right, my thoughts are all my own!

You're surprised? Who else would want that thought?

Lewis Carrol did something similar!

You're entitled to your opinion.

Ah, my opinions are my own as well?

Yes and you can give them away, even sell them, that is, if anybody thinks them valuable, or keep them to yourself.

Well then, why are you so free with *your* opinions?

I don't have opinions, I know.

Then why am I continually reading and hearing, "God says this and God wants that"?

You sound more than a bit angry. Much better to direct your irritation towards those who seek to bolster their opinions by pretending they're mine, rather than towards me.

Anyone who presents his opinion as though it were yours, is wrong?

Not necessarily, but one could easily suspect that he wanted to bolster his prejudices, that he hadn't done his homework, that his argument was weak, or quite simply, that deep down he had little confidence in himself.

Are you referring to me?

If the shoe fits—

I thought you were my friend?

So I am—but you were talking about freedom to think, freedom to express an opinion—just had the idea that it might be relevant.

You have ideas?

Of course. What do you suppose I do with all that I know? Just leave it fallow in my memory? God—the vast data bank of the universe?

What ideas do you have then?

What do you imagine?

You're pretty good when it comes to answering a question with another question.

What's wrong with that if it helps you to realise that you know more than you think you do? So, brush up your imagination. With it you can leap walls.

At a single bound? Who d'you think I am—Superman?

Not at all. I know you too well for that. Super friend perhaps; and one endowed with intelligence, feeling and creative imagination.

I'm not *you*. How should *I* know the ideas you might think up?

No need to be indignant. Haven't you got everything

that exists in your head?

I've got *you* in my head. Sometimes I wish I hadn't.

And the universe?

Well, if *you're* in my head, I suppose I've got to say that I've got the whole universe there as well! It's absurd. One of your crazy paradoxes again.

You're not convinced? Shut your eyes. What do you see?

A lot of specks that look like stars.

Are they stars?

Of course they aren't.

Keep looking, but imagine that they are stars. What do you see now?

I see the night sky.

Is there a moon?

Uh—might be—there are some clouds. There *could* be a moon hiding itself behind the clouds. Yes, I see it now. It's three quarters full. Venus is setting on the right.

Sure it's Venus? Perhaps it's another star system altogether?

Another star system? Come to think of it the moon does look a strange colour. Oh, there's a second moon. A bit smaller. And a huge planet with a triple ring system!

Two moons and a huge triple-ringed planet. Where are you?

God knows!

Right, I do. You're in your head. Your imagination.

What did you want to remind me for? That was a great trip!

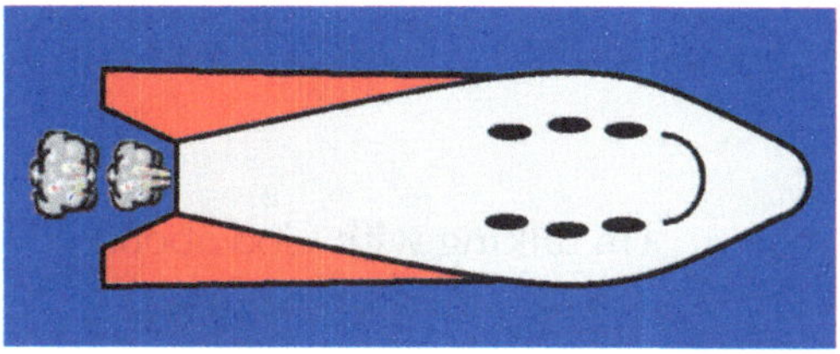

Glad you enjoyed it. You can go there again whenever you like. Now, back to my original question. What do you imagine I think about?

About how to keep one up on me!

Not bad, you help keep me on my toes. And—?

How to improve your creation without infringing your creation's thoughts and opinions.

Evolution? That's a good one. And—?

Developing improved communications?

Spot on! and—?

How to encourage shared management?

Getting ambitious, are we?

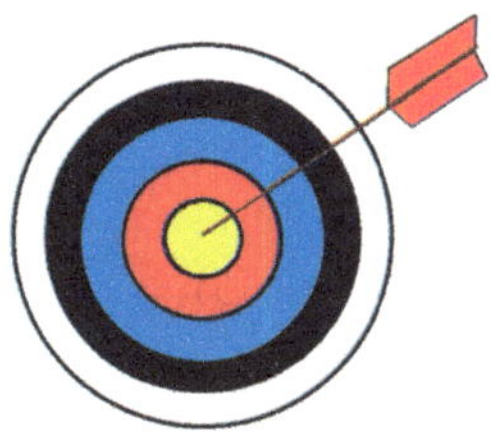

The opportunity's too good to miss.

It's noted. And—?

Improved data management?

Sounds very up to date. But you already mentioned communications.

Data is the raw information that passes over the communication links.

01110000100010000111000101110010

Just testing.

Hey is this really happening?

I'm talking with God about
management of the universe?
It's completely over the top!

Don't get too excited. Remember this is your imagination at work. Actually not a lot to do with me, unless from it emerges substantive or directed thought, belief, or action.

You mean my imagi-
nation is mine, to do
what I like with?

Your very own. You can do your personal creating with it—in a small way of course—no actual matter involved, but even so, it's extremely powerful.

Is that why the Bible
Says you created man
in your own image?[5]

You didn't understand it to mean something else, surely?

Er—

You don't have to answer—I know already.

[5] Genesis 1:27: "So God created man in his own image, in the image of God he created him; male and female he created them."

Your move...
P-STJ

P-St J
GB-JB

The Author

The London-born author has had a varied career beginning, shortly after the Second World War, as a military pilot. On leaving the Royal Air Force, he became a Chartered Engineer working in aerospace research. This work took him to Woomera in the Australian desert, to four years' residence in Paris and to the European Space Centre in French Guiana.

On returning to Australia, the author entered a partnership for the preparation of technical manuals. He had a short spell as an examiner of patents, before joining the Royal Australian Navy as a civilian in a project management team.

Sometime later, the Australian Senate began restructuring its committee system and the author found himself appointed Secretary to the Australian Senate Standing Committee on Science and the Environment. Eight years later, after having prepared parliamentary reports on eleven major public inquiries, he was recruited to join the staff of the Australian Science and Technology Advisory Council reporting to the Prime Minister.

During this time he became interested in the work of the Inter-Parliamentary Union, based in Geneva. The Union, established in 1889, works to foster peace through parliamentary action as well as to help strengthen parliamentary democracy throughout the world. Prominent members of the Union have won the Nobel Peace Prize on eight occasions. The author, recruited in 1984, was responsible, amongst other activities, for managing the library and supervising the Union's regular publications.

As a writer, he has prepared numerous technical papers and reports including a two-volume reference compendium on the parliaments of the world. Eight novels have also come from his hand.

He now lives in France where, from retirement he is active in a cultural association for the promotion of creative activities.

He has a son, two grandsons, a great-grandson and a great-granddaughter.

For more information visit
www.peterstjohn.net

Lightning Source UK Ltd.
Milton Keynes UK
UKOW06f1024080515

251149UK00010B/62/P

9 781781 323960